twinkle-tree

A play-a-long story for His glory

by Corinne Badenhorst

Twinkle-Tree

For your copy of Twinkle tree - please contact Corinne at 0836605412 or avontconnect@gmail.com

Story and Illustration by Corinne Badenhorst.

Published by Seraph Creative in 2019.

ISBN 978-0-620-83263-2

Published by

SeraphCreative

Heaven's Heart for Earth

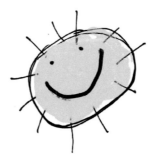

A play-a-long story for His glory

his allegory is based on an answered prayer.

n image from heaven which God attached to my heart.

itter has a magical feel to it - and so has the kingdom of God. Glitter sembles the ways and fruit of God. It is with "glitter" that heaven and earth timately integrates and come together as Light, a mighty but gentle force.

n allegory that hopefully changes perspectives, helps us to not integrate e's conflicts and people's behaviour into our identity, but rather default to e "Magic" within us.

his allegory aims to plant a seed of resilience in each and every reader's heart so that our focus can shift from the outer world to the greatness within.

Corinne Badenhorst

B. Occupational Therapy 2001

Long, long, Lóóóng ago,
even before the creation of the
world***
You were already a delightful
piece of art in GOD's heart!♥

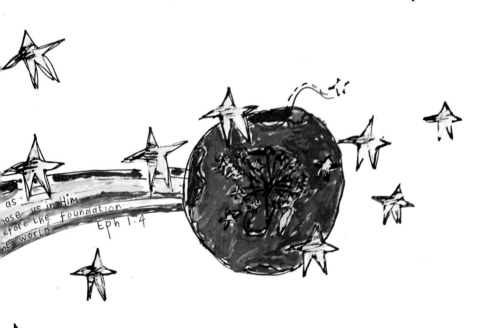

 as
ose us in Him
efore the foundation
he world   Eph 1.4

He marked your Birthdate
on His majestic
time-card*
Everything about you perfectly
set-apart.

In the vaults of your DNa---
He hid a Very   special
                    story,

for you to discover and
  use for His Glory*!

plans
of peace
not evil
a future
and

expectancy
Jer 29:11

Behind a little door of
your heart ; He concealed a
Heavenly-treasure
            valuable and smart.

What is this treasure?

A twinkle-tree //
that will grow and grow
and grow₉₉₉*
It is exactly what this
tree does.
It brings heaven and earth
closer together
in your heart.

NoW ~ Guess What grows
from your twinkle-tree?

GLitter!

that shimmers and
shines with a Bright
sparkling Light..
* --- almost like little mirrors from Heaven —*

It glitters and shines pieces
of Heaven in your heart...
it makes all things
B·e·a·u·t·i·f·u·L —
♡ just the way love always does ♡

♡-glitter is light as a
feather ;
it can come-to-rest a·n·y·where
like a fly-balloon does ✩✩✩

It is Lionhearted ;
forgives simply...
is packed with heaps of love.
radiates the colours of the rainbow ;
tickles your heart with jo

and Flutters around like a
1000 Butterflies
when you smile |
✩

the glitter of your heart
will unfailingly spark and
Never depart ,
                because it
     mirrors and shines heaven
   in your heart ...
It is your Lifestory that
  proclaims that
You , are You , are You ➡
       the Best and only You !

But...

Sometimes a friend might feel a little "short-and-sharp"; he probably forgot to guard his heart.

,,, and before he knows,
a few prickles grows.
His twinkle-tree is no
     Longer Free ---

,, I am ANGRY, Very, Very
          ANGRY ! ,,
    You may hear a prickle
                  say ...

Prickles éééasily grow
all over and around his
twinkle-tree,
and prickles prick —
that's what prickles
DÓ...

It's so painful that he will try a·a·anything to make the prick-prick-prick stop.

---Even to scratch and hurt his friend---

When someone so much as
tickles his prickles ,,,

oh Woe !

What a painful
happening .

the prickles prick, scratch
and hurt his heart —
then his mouth goes all the
way to say:

"GO away! I don't want
to play!
You can't and you should not"

Prickles sting like a Bee!
   they never miss a thing...
,,, But, if you remember
what a ♥prickle does ---
   you will never ever e·v·e·r
become like BitterWing Doodle
      or his side-kick
   PrickLY PurpLe PoodLe!

No, you will only twinkle
and know....,
,,I touched a prickle today."

But GOD fashioned my heart
stronger than Goliath ...
<u>right</u> from the start ;

remember...

You may talk
about a friend's
♡-prickles ---

and absolutely say:

"Here is a glitter for you
dear friend, as I sense a prickle
in your heart ...
Be brave, very brave and quickly
pull it out,
otherwise you
might loose your
friend."

then... Above e·v·e·ry·thing —
take good care of your own
twinkle-tree
More than any other treasure
or even your kitty-cat's
pLeasUre...!

Because this is exactly how the
secrets of your Life-story are to
be found ... ☆

Open up your twinkle-tree and
Let your glitter free.——⭐
that is how a piece of Heaven
can come to earth for you
and Me.

Glitter is the heavenly-mirrors of your
twinkle-tree. Find it! Explore with it and
share it — this way it will become more
and more and more — and even be like
a plaster on a friend's prickly-sore.

then dear friend ...

then you have a
superstarglitterheart ...
- and that is magical and smart -

About Corinne

Corinne is a seeker of the depths, truths and treasures to be found in God's heart, a wife, a mom and an Occupational therapist.

avontconnect@gmail.com

083 660 5412

"Write down my Glitter"

Let your friends write down which
"glitter" they receive from you...

"Because that is how you let pieces of Heaven stay with them"

Draw your Twinkle Tree

Teach Your Children to Live From Heaven!

Seraph is honoured to present amazing, high quality books to remind today's children where they came from, who they are and what they can do as Sons of God.

These are the books we wish we had!

Visit our website:
www.seraphcreative.org

Made in the USA
Las Vegas, NV
06 September 2022

54613319R00029